Stealing Mercury

*For Tanis,
my not-so-imaginary
new writing friend.* — Lori
Oct 2005

Stealing Mercury

Lori Cayer

[signature]
04/21/04

© 2004, Lori Cayer

All rights reserved. No part of this book may be reproduced, stored in a retrieval system or transmitted in any form or by any means without written permission from The Muses' Company, an imprint of J. Gordon Shillingford Publishing Inc., except for brief excerpts used in critical reviews, for any reason, by any means, without the permission of the publisher.

The Muses' Company Series Editor: Catherine Hunter
Cover art is entitled "Jusstice" by Jody Hudey and incorprates a photograph by Gene Johnson (used with permission of Getty Images)
Book design by Terry Gallagher/Doowah Design Inc.
Author photo by Shannon Kennedy
Printed and bound in Canada

We acknowledge the financial support of the Manitoba Arts Council and The Canada Council for the Arts for our publishing program.

"Ayaz and the King's Pearl" from *The Essential Rumi*. Translations by Coleman Barks with John Moyne, Castle Books, 1997.

"Sunrise" from Mary Oliver's *New and Selected Poems*, Beacon Press, Boston, 1992.

Canadian Cataloguing in Publication Data

Cayer, Lori
    Stealing mercury/Lori Cayer.
Poems.
ISBN 0-920486-65-7

I. Title.
PS8605.A94S84 2004   C811'.6   C2004-901431-5

J. Gordon Shillingford Publishing
P.O. Box 86, RPO Corydon Avenue, Winnipeg, MB Canada R3M 3S3

Table of Contents

Miscellaneous Anatomy

Silver Map / 11
Raising a Child With Hemophilia / 14
Today He Is a Poet / 17
Bleeder / 18
Death's Early Colours Are All We Know of Spring / 19
Amateur's Guide to Agoraphobia / 21
Eulogizing the Cat / 23
The Broken Among Us / 24
What the Right Hand Doesn't Know / 26
In the Bush with Him / 28
Why I Stopped Watching Surgery / 30

The Body Received

Codeine Dreams / 33
The Body Received / 38
Mapping the Drive / 40
To the One Searching My Body: A Duet / 42

Breathing Clouds

Killing Tammy / 47
Imprint of the Mother / 51
Mother Road / 53
Just Ask Her / 55
Pictures of Me Not Even Bothering / 57
A Consolation of Lilacs / 60
Her Dream is the Water / 64

The Sky I've Made

Small Town Desire / 69
Termination of View 1 / 70
Lesbian Scenarios You Don't Think About / 72
Your Letter: 5 Translations / 73
Some Notes Toward Drowning / 77
The Middles of Our Conversations / 78
Return Address / 79
Termination of View 2 / 81
Epilogue: / 82

Bloodblossom

Line of Questioning / 85
Stealing Mercury / 86
Starting Now / 88
There Have Been Mornings Like This / 90
Verge / 91
Two Solitudes / 93
My Morning Body / 94
Bloodblossom / 95

The Animals That Inhabit Him

The Animals That Inhabit Him / 99

Acknowledgements / 112

A hundred thousand impressions from the spirit
are wanting to come through here.
                              I feel stunned
in this abundance, crushed and dead.

                    Rumi

What is the name
of the deep breath I would take
over and over
for all of us? Call it

whatever you want, it is
happiness, it is another one
of the ways to enter
fire.
                              Mary Oliver

Miscellaneous Anatomy

Silver Map

my son suggests I cast my eyes
higher than I've ever looked before

up to the roof of Westminster United
        its angular shingles

the sheer colour of a rainless
but overcast day

        he is up there
holding on to nothing

hovering, floating—
a drum-skin kite tethered to the bell tower

that night I dreamed
I climbed a mountain
fingernails grinding into rock
trees close together as an embrace
until I was breathless and the closeness
was stone and I was
mining my way to the top

in the morning I change his secret name
I will call him

Spider-Boy:
the story of his thirteenth year a kind

of ecstasy, a clamouring in his sleek head
compelling him to do

something amazing
with his speechless body

and so each evening he climbs
the limestone

body of the church
arms and legs angled and sticky

without fear he walks the rain-gutter
negotiates every silver pitch—

for that roof is many roofs locked
together in a puzzle—

until he reaches the bell tower

and there he holds himself
against the loom of the empty air

he stays until the dusk pours
over him

until someone in a uniform
makes him come down

another morning after dreaming
I will show him
the church that I see, my eyes
locked on the rose
window, its red and blue circuitry
a divine x-ray of a boy's body
spinning downward
and emptying into the grass

now he is landlocked—dreams
he is the kite dreams he is

the wind above a city dreams
he is alone on a silver map

this is the translation I receive:
architect, cartographer

he draws it for me
with a soft black pencil

traces his spidery route
a white ritual he repeats

from memory
folded and slipped under my door

Raising a Child with Hemophilia:
A Practical Guide for Parents
— A found poem

bruises and bleeds:
do:
sew foam padding into clothing
outline a new bruise with pen dots
to see if it is spreading

dark red is a sign

ask questions
a great deal depends upon the answers

the body can experience
joint bleeds muscle bleeds major bleeds
also minor and severe bleeds
throat and neck
head and eye
gastrointestinal
bleeds

when injured
he will not bleed faster
only longer

remember
child abuse accusations can almost
seem a way of life

treatment:
your son's natural reaction is to scream
when being held down

you will learn
the skin is thin
finding a vein is very hard

keep this in mind
not the idea that your son is being tortured

do not:
over-react
the last thing you need
is more people crying

daredevil syndrome:
the denier may ignore a bleed that is occurring

your son demands freedom
he wants desperately

as a teen he may adopt risky behaviour
attempt dangerous activities

it is completely normal to fear this
when the time comes

you must cease rushing into situations
making explanations

he will not be a baby
anymore

it is more like your son is missing

overprotection:
be prepared
your sense of failure can be overwhelming

you may feel guilt and sadness
to your core
this will be very hard on him

he resents

being a constant reminder
of human frailty

we do not choose
a future which seems frightening
a sudden, unexpected turn of events

certainly not this
obscure
disorder

shock may be the briefest emotion
you experience

Today He Is a Poet

when his tangerine heart
is eleven
he watches them cut open
a woman on the Learning Channel
belly of the blade sinking a thick
red hole big enough
for two hands to slip in
pull out a glistening blue turkey
the smiling mother doesn't feel a thing
he admires
her pale blue gift
wants to tell her about the hole
collapsed and steaming so close
she should be able to smell
her own heart beating
he learns it takes an hour
and a half to have a baby that way
but it's mostly sewing

he tells me he would write
what scares him
cancer like a lobster head stuck
at an angle, an arrowhead lodged
in his narrow body
the shadow-dancers in his room
only he doesn't know how to spell
the words
his heart keeps him awake at night
a supple bruise in his chest keening
the river of its soft alarm
he begins to walk the ragged edge
insomnia's loose alphabet of stones
asking unanswerable questions until morning

Bleeder

he wants to be an accident
for Hallowe'en
the year I insist he join Cub Scouts
luckily, we have all the stuff
the little crutches from the time
his unstoppable blood
moored him to the couch
an old neck brace
some rolls of gauze

I consider
the four severed pumpkins
on the hearth awaiting
a second, more brutal death
the knife and melted wax
the things we do to scare ourselves

we buy blood from a package
that clots faster than the fine
thin nectar travelling
beneath his lucent skin
he adds the tan uniform and beret
for ironic effect

I don't tell him I'm afraid
of his heart ticking backwards
like an oven-timer
that every night I dream
his mangled bike, a fire
a car crushed like tinfoil
and now, this bleeding
costume at my door
holding out its bag of candy

he is standing
just outside my reach
where the elms in autumn
form a long yellow hallway
and the anxious wind is always
just arriving

Death's Early Colours Are All We Know of Spring

1.
I'm on my way to a party, warm wind
from the open window exaggerating my hair
warm sun the only promise

at Portage and Broadway
the squeegee kids hitch
their eyes to me   mother
citizen   richlady
in my ten-year-old car and my discount dress

I give them nothing every day
what they ask for opens
a pain low in my belly
uterine, it reminds me who I am
then cramps and closes its fist
all my coins hoarded
to feed my own disquieted boy

this is spring on the prairies
though they stand there in winter too
soldiers waiting for orders
in battered army boots, wrecked runners
box-board sign stating the obvious
(cold and hungry)
of course you are

perhaps you know my son
he has an address right now, a phone number
some techniques for paying the rent

2.
here on the prairies, death's early colours
are all we know of spring
browns and greys, leached
grass and concrete, load of dust forgotten
in the streets by water's sudden absence

parents of other children speed by in their cars
windows closed and dirty
when the light is red adjust the radio
count the seconds to green
they are afraid of something coming too close
of paying for something they didn't want to buy

I can't feed all of you
I won't give them my parking money
they won't sleep at home
we each have our reasons for holding back

3.
running behind time, I pass them by

and when I see him
with the other kids (the doppelgänger's children)
working the corner, working
the reds for spare change
      I see a boy, both lost and found

I am his mother and the mother of them all
make no mistake
I am an accessory after the fact

there are groceries in his apartment
he will come for dinner Sunday
he does not see me driving by
between my teeth a taste of metal and dust

looking worn out and hot
in his best t-shirt and worst shoes, dragging
his borrowed squeegee behind him like a pull-toy
like a leash without a dog
he does not see me driving by

I go to the party without turning back
I go without saying

Amateur's Guide to Agoraphobia

1.
early notes indicate the laziness of spring
the branches are waiting—I didn't know we had finches
a sparrow crochets its way through last year's grass
under and through, under and through

indoors the radio is a barking lunatic
from my menu of personal options I choose silence
staying in on a beautiful day is more
and less, a constant under and through

I cross the chasm of inches to my office
the cats are a posse of sycophants
their sedulous needs an annoying delight
they root me (under and through)

I choose to stand, elbows on the sill
translating the conversation of crows
the only word I'm sure of—
cat! cat! cat! cat!

passing under their tree

2.
the computer makes a faraway trill
like those starlings in Japan
that mimic the ringing of cell phones

can one get away with
sedulous and *sycophant*
in the same sentence?

I'm in the kitchen in my nightclothes
cutting recipes out of magazines
measuring windows for curtains

making lists
making
lists

3.
the crows shred the sunlight
patrol their city, are never
misled by the acres of mirrors
their black radar certain
of that which is a tree

and that which is water-skim
flashed-back picture of a tree
a half-crazed woman
with a pair of scissors deep
in its ragged branches

4.
every day at least one bird hits
at least one window of this house

yesterday two at once
a couple dancing

the sound of their bodies on the glass
trust   trust

dysphoria of morning
their dance paralyzed by light

Eulogizing the Cat

you open yourself to me like a jacket
show your white lining
now I see you
and the surgeon's disappearing hand

snow-angel, swimmer
my question, the asking of it
opens you like an eye, opens
you like a suitcase full of fruit

your body floods, contracts
breathes breathes
dark red tongue of spleen a ribbon
snipped and set before me

this doctor's work is nothing
so much as sewing—
a biological standing-up to reason
an attempt at survival

we can both believe in
I won't say my being there was a gift
but it was
your tumour of tatted lace, friable

unknotted, undone
this auctioning-off of your
blood's belongings, my last chance
to attend you with my need

body closed, blue eyes closed
deep ether of your breath a kind of
living, your light wanes
leaving you in its incubator

the clock perseveres through the night
at dawn I feel the light leaving you
leaving this room
heading for home

The Broken Among Us

he is a boy kissing his new baby
lightly on the lips
kisses like
hummingbird touches to a flower
that delicate and brief
that meaningful

the world has been anxious
to call him a man, call him Daddy
when he hasn't one of his own
call him to task
for his mistakes—already full-grown
and chasing him down like dogs

this nephew is a boy like my son
some days surprised
to be barely past the age of twenty
completely awake
and beginning to realize
things are exactly as they seem

he is a boy with a theory
I can appreciate:
Hell is a hospital, he says
where the broken among us go
not for punishment
      but for repair
something like mercy for the accidents
of our lives

his chaste gesture
disassembles
the overcrowded peony of my heart
petals abscising—falling all at once
an expiration, a collapse
its burden of beauty and sorrow
too heavy

he is a man

with the uncurling blossom
of his son's body in his two hands
he is a boy lit
with the strange hellfire
of possibility

What the Right Hand Doesn't Know

the left hand will not tell, it wakes you from a bloody
shocking dream, where you're still my Dad, but

find yourself in hospital, flipping things over
in your mind, the motor running, still running

your good hand glyphs a question, repeats
the question of your wife: *what were you thinking?*

been starting that obstinate compressor
that way for years, gave it a pull same as any day

then you stood there alone
in your wood-shop—

five minutes to supper time
the grand-kids waiting in their chairs

—stunned. stunning. this wronged hand not
even bleeding yet, the pause between heartbeats

half your life, blades and machines and not one
accident, then this—motor, pulleys and the belt

that snakes tight between them, so fast
…your fingers

the pink astonishment of your fingers flying like
baby birds, like flesh sparks

landing here and there in the sawdust
remnants, embers quickly cooling

your daughters, sent to collect them
scan the floor on hands and knees for three

fingers without a hand, gather them
in a clean cloth, feel the schism

the rupture in the credulous skin of the future
supper gone cold on the table

by the time you drove yourself to the hospital
your rag-wrapped hand was a torch, pumping red

a fist full of fire beating its way toward surprise
toward the rest of the story: the damage too great

so your hand must learn to forget them,
your very own fingers—nesting in your pocket

closing around any idea you could clasp, hammer
or mitre into place, your hand waking you

in the night, counting on two fingers the limitations
of surgery, of codeine

of pain like a motor running
an absence that will not be ignored—listen

to the way it comes rapping
white as a sheet before dawn

In the Bush with Him

on winter Saturdays he took us out
leaving an angry mother in the hot house, jealous
animal keeping to her den
not willing to be caught dead
tramping around in the bush
freezing her feet for nothing

she is tired of it all—
his preferring the company of the kids
the bootfuls of snow, the hunt

he took us out
a stiff-legged, overdressed trail of ducklings
ice fishing all day—
all flat white brittle day—
the four of us standing around the long hole
augered down
through the middle of perilous nothing
keep moving, he'd say, *jump around
and you'll warm up*

I don't recall the fish

he took us out, following the deer trails
that curved and bent between the bare legs
of the poplars, past the crones of scrub-oak
rabbit, he'd say, pointing
with his bow-and-arrow hand
at the pellets in the snow
we were meant to learn something about hunger
something essential he could tell us only here
in the quiet room of his forest
where everything was catalogued
and understandable

I recall the rabbits hanging like red scarves

in the back porch, his bow-and-arrow hand
now a knife
he took us out, brought us back in time
for Bugs Bunny, Mom mashing the potatoes
with the electric mixer on high
mad about the rabbits, about him, about us
conductivity dragging the TV reception
in jerky patterns toward the kitchen

he took us out into the weatherless days
so we might see
what he sees in the black and white frame
of winter, his picture of life
oxidized, pending
so we might know the feel of the bow
rising, the strong arm pulling back
the impossibly stretched cord

I recall the rabbits
running like snow

Why I Stopped Watching Surgery

I take it all back
the body's
red machine hurts me now
I am no longer brave and
curious
when I see the glistening knot of bone

this is what a knee looks like
the waxy fabric
of skin snipped and folded
pinned and basted, a kind

of snappy domesticity, motherly
taking down of pants, surprise
of white bum
this joint in its wet hole

is this all we can make of dying
this third eye looking
inward?
some sort of
flower so full-blown it shoves its insides
out

The Body Received

Codeine Dreams

4:40 a.m.
                        (codeine comes at night
                         tapping out a message
a series of   small   white   naps)

I am detained by this life-saving—
                after days spent in the hospital
my hair feels like it smells, like a damp box
                from a damp corner of basement

all I want is near enough to ask for
                (codeine's
                undivided attention
                peaceful sleep
                gift of de tachment)

my elderly neighbour is mostly blind
her half-life in her horse-stall bed
she thinks everyone's come to see her

who's   there?
                a metronome's query
who's   there?

4:15 a.m.
winter arrives while I'm sleeping
my lover comes and goes as if under water
                as if he's lost me under water
and must now swim home alone

(codeine dreams
                you can hear the dreamnoise all night long)
the sound of your life moving back and forth
                down the wide halls
                pushed along on metal wheels

(codeine dreams it has visitors
from outside
appalling din of normalcy)
deposits in the bank of regular time

4:51 a.m.
who's   there?
lost and found
       insecurity?

                no dear, it's not lost
                it's in security
                it's four in the morning
                you should try to sleep

cormorant, gull, the unknown spirit of me
skimming a galvanized surface of water
my own flat planet

        (between naps, between my lover's visits
I become imaginary)

I keep a spangled eye on my intravenous girlfriend
thin drink of medicated water, she is chrome, silverfished
she is assigned to save my life
gives me blood thinner
her long hair the colour of plastic tubing
        she enters me
        she follows me like the dog she is

4:35 a.m.
        things you can do in the hospital
        at four in the morning:
        get blood taken
        answer the fifty questions of yet
        another student
        watch the guy with the unconscious fever
        receive a high speed kind of bath
        from a spray bottle
        three nurses are needed to
        cool his overheated flesh
        spritz and turn, tumble and dry

        hospital things go on without you

                    (codeine thinks how easy it would be
                    to stop time
                    to become in valid)

dreamwhite nap in a half-lit pond
a strangeness—
washing my
self
in the sheets of my bed
a basin of cloudy water
                    wee canoe of soap
                    afloat

4:56 a.m.
my lover brings a gift
what else can he do
                    they call me his wife

I am not the same girl he came here with
he thinks the word
                    ramifications

takes it with him to the silt-blind bottom
of despair

winter settles over the still-moving water
(in my empty hand
a bottle of tiny naps, silver-plated and just
                    under the surface
                    of sound)

4:25 a.m.
                    one more thing you can do in the hospital
                    at four a.m.: listen
                    as your helpless neighbour gets weighed
                         crashing, clanging horrid iron frame
                         they drop and drop the parts, then
                    finally get the old lady dangled
                    in her storksack for all of fifteen seconds
                    then do it all again backwards
                    not in the least deaf, she says predictably

>   *who's there?*
>   *it must be Jesus Christ*
>   *I can tell it's him, by the sound of his cane*

4:12 a.m.
my lover brings curry
hot and late
I eat it with my hands and he stays
until I sleep

>   (codeine is my reward for pain
>   if I want it
>   it is near enough)

the whole of my life a series
of movements toward arrival
toward beginning a story already half over

4:24 a.m.
>   they tell me
>   this blood thinner
saving my so-called life
and the life of my so-called
husband

is used to kill rodents
no repellent, this substance
>   takes up the bodies of the unwanted
>   loves them from the inside, waters down
>   the blood till the organs liquefy
thins mine so I do not become lodged
forever in time
stroked out
stuck tick-tocking *who's there who's there*

>   (codeine is my brain's white lie
>   aphasia—
>   a kind of privacy—
>   protects me
>   from words I thought I knew)

something something like a horse and carriage…

4:59 a.m.
                      (every four hours
                      codeine comes for me and
                      I   just
                      drift   away)

delaying what I will soon remember—
I must still love
my
self

enough
the body, the head: the sorrowful machine
they have become

to go home, begin the story again

I must still love my   self
        (imagine)
the surprise found in that
the imperative

The Body Received

it's some kind of luck to suffer pain so easily
       its signal hammering through the wall
of complacence
warning me of an outcome worse than dying

worse than heartbreak
worse than old and alone
than just taking my foot off the brake
any of those days I wanted to
       edge of high speed traffic
            route 90 at rush hour

pain in the neckjawfaceheadscalpeye
much, much bigger than codeine
an eye like a camera lens—pupil shutting
down, f-stopping its way out of business

doctor number five said…could have stroked out
       burst blot
of blood like a fertilized egg dropped
       in the cookie dough (surprise)
could have been left with nothing
       but breathing
a giant baby, needing that much care
       just breathing with no language in
       no language out
or even dead
all my language a nutmeat, cold in my head

pain a high voltage cord, a runner bean
       of vein and nerve
one thread, a way to die bleeding
the other a way to live   unexpecting

I was caught in time

alive and mostly well, I backtrack
through my body's peculiar days
study its interior terrain

from books have memorized the Latin
that makes language
of the inscrutable meat
of the body
six months healing carotid artery
aperture of eye
narrowed for good

      I see my self on film
beautiful tumour-free brain
torn artery, optic nerve

all roads lead north
where the headache watches over me
a lighthouse flashing the way

a map to lead me
past breathing
all the way to night

Mapping the Drive

the minutiae of my headache
        I have to say
cannot be compared to the weather
to migraine's turban of broken glass
and spin
           it cannot be compared
though the wind is constantly killing me
with its cold knives
        binary, ambidextrous
suckling my only breath
like a cat got into the cradle

narcotic exactitude pleases me

this headache is a destination
rare but charted
this pain is a file corrupted
alluvium of Latinate words
unilateral
        nonthrobbing ischemia

all of this is transparently true
fifteen small meals on hospital time
carotid dissection pressing
hypoglossal nerve
review of systems is otherwise normal

these days my headache is who I am
        (how I am frequently
lost in my own city, its old habit of roads)
it is the stick holding up the split
blossom of my head
radiant peony *(paeonia lactiflora)*
it is the sun's soprano laser
particulating the unprepared eye

I carry on, you know I do
        peculiar and diffuse
my drugs a monologue
of bifurcate names
yellow, yellow, blue
and finally
I duck the ipsilateral bruise of my head
under the low bridge of sleep
Ctrl Alt Delete
        yellow, blue, blue, sleep

To the One Searching My Body: A Duet

at first my body resists you
though you are only trying to help
release my vertebrae like birds
from a magician's hands
my sorrow eludes you
but you continue panning, digging
fingers inserted to the first knuckle

she seems unable to speak, to protect herself
        though you are
among the gentlest
of men

over my head
your bluesky window
wears a bullet hole in its lapel
like a lover, I leave myself in your care

     comfort her
         with feathers

I have heard you will give yourself as a gift
to anyone who needs the pinking light
of sunrise
I appeal to you, the owner of all
the therapies, submit
the plate tectonics of my skull, my spine
a rundown street

     mouth, sacrum, the impossible
absorption of pink
     light

the tenor of your whispered voice
comforts me like feathers
my sorrow is a settling
of coins in synovial pockets
is the water beneath your dowser's query

> *she has gathered*
> *stones in her pocket*
> > *bruisings of memory*

ultrasound, radar
the weight of your medical hand
finds the black box:
a memory of long gone spring
the smell of my hair woody and sharp
like something unexpected from the garden

your diligence
> *abbreviates her, opens*
her like an egg
geiger   static   hum
> *a starburst of cracks*

an ending in stony increments
the one I love disappearing into the sky
for the last time
with no understanding, whatsoever, of blue

> *synaptic output*
> > *she is opening*

your fingers are:
a green willow cradle among other things
a tripod of burning candles, a picket fence
holding the morning nest of my head
my broken neck a bird's orgasm

the end of flight, a starburst of cracks
a neural sky
opens para-sympathetically over
> *a gift of stones*
> *and feathers*
my unsuspecting body
like walking on air toward home
the sky a blue window
the sky an explosion of glass
> *the colour of her body's*
> *light*

Breathing Clouds

Killing Tammy

I am catching her collapse
        just then
taking her down when
        the front door opens
mother home from work
and here's Tammy   dead
on my mom's bedside mat

it's only a game

a game with one rule:
don't get seen don't get caught
        just the two of us and the blinding swoon
that binds our bodies
one girl big, the other small
it is sex and drugs before we know them
        it is cloister

memory drops from the sky like
        stone bird star
some known thing
still capable of surprise

Tammy is a hungry
girl like me
        knows how to keep a secret
the game is the glow that inhabits me
        like an idea, like a hand on fire
quivering and impossible to put down

picture: two girls standing single file
the game begins this way
body touching body   closeness
the one in front
        held and compliant begins
the ritual of breathing
ten gut-deep breaths counted out loud
hyper   hyper   vent
ilate

the one behind tightens her arms around
the chest of the other
a clasp like lifesaving, fist hard as a heart
tucked up and under the ribs
both hands
ready to push the heart-fist
in and up
on the tenth held breath

hold her breath hold her body
until the breather falls
fast
in a swoon
asphyxia deliria
dead or alive
the faller cannot care

I am doing it to her and she falls
not three steps from the safety
of my own doorclosing room
      she falls like a deadgirl
she falls like a bag of wet cement
I am starved, insubstantial
a styrofoam girl
in love with Tammy

the point is, when your turn comes
      you are going to fall
a speculation of stars
and she will be there
to catch you
to lay you out cold

the game does not end when you fall
the closed eyes of the moon watch you
hang in the universe on a wire
oxygen-starved blood
throwing cold sparks off frozen bones

breathing becomes blue stars and
               (listen)   distant
voice of your friend
     does it feel good?
and your runaway heart wants to say
the best   the best

we are in my mother's room
where we have not been allowed to play
since we gave the styrofoam wig-head
its true face
eyeshadowed expression of suffocation
watching us
watching me kill Tammy
a lesson in permanence that
did not sink in   and now

here's Tammy on the mat not waking
        up and my mom is on the stairs
and Tammy is not
        waking up
I try to drag her body from the room but
she is the biggest mistake I have ever made and
        she's heavy

I learn about the point
        of no return
Tammy learns about it too
my mom   gets to the top of the stairs
and
        Tammy wakes up
my mom gets to the top of the stairs and

sees me and Tammy smiling our wig-head smiles
in the middle of her doorway
        says
what the hell are you two up to
and goes into her room
to change out of her work clothes
her nyloned feet none-the-wiser
standing on the tufted mat of death

      I grow up, maybe
become a woman with a list
of those who will claim to have
been my lovers
a collision of gestures
death or utopia
an odd-numbered list of attempts

and if I see Tammy
say, in twenty years
in a bookstore studying astrology
I might ask if she remembers
        the arms of a girl around her
        the absolute failure of flight
the smell of popping lightbulbs
falling stars

that black craving
speeding
at the rate of memory
circling in the dark
              where the aging moon
      still hovers
eating up all the air

Imprint of the Mother

the summer before the snakes came
for me, my father packed us into the brown
Pontiac for a day beside one of the million
lakes I thought of as his private stock
another and another flat blue

dime on the green blanket of prairie
how my mother despised those trips
wrenched from the safety of her clean house
to hurtle with him and the damned kids
down gritty yellow roads, down

to where the snakes lived
we'd stand up three girls in a row
to watch my mother expertly hurl her
glass coke bottle far into the ditch
the cigarette in her other

hand not even quivering
and always she'd say *get off
the back of my neck for God's sake*
but really she meant
stand away from her perfect

corolla, the spun brown-sugar flower
of her delicate hair
when we'd get to my father's lake
she would stay in the car until he insisted
she come out and have lunch and somehow

her thonged brown feet would
cross the terrible sand and grass
mottled snake-hiding terrain between
car and picnic table
where she would sit the long bright

day with her feet on the bench smoking
her left-handed cigarette
I understand now the space made by gifts
circles of blue, squares of green
those wanted and those impressed

upon us, the simple offerings of my father
because the next summer, along with walnuts
of perfect pain pushing like seedlings from my thin
white chest, came my mother's gift—
her weakness sliding down

on me, my small world forever divided
like a skipping rope lounging
across a hot road one step from before
into every day after, dreaming
one impossible step back
to an unblighted *before* black
and yellow elongated narrow
tube of skin became
imprinted on my retina
my translucent feet on the green

susurration of grass
meant snake coming out of nowhere
back to those seamless days when three girls
tumbled in the broad back seat breathing clouds
of fine prairie dust, still young

enough to demand
occasional moments of dread
asking him to drive faster over the gravelled hills
our hearts flying up
like cabbage moths into our throats

Mother Road
— a found poem of book titles

who dies, curing disease with food
all the anxious girls on earth
        hunting down home
the truth [is] wherever you go
there you are
feeling good in the belly of the
beast, coping with panic
        the mother dance
the spiral
way [of] gifts differing

the woman beneath the skin
 [a] girl interrupted
look[s] back in anger
shame and guilt
always a body to trade
        sisters
motherless daughters
breath dances between them

a breath from elsewhere
        running in the family
[in the] fractured
mirror, the refiner's fire
        you are here, sitting in the fire
[a] wild woman dancing the dreams
of the body
conquering pain, solitude
[and] revenge

heal your life [in]
the circle of care
making soap at home
focussing
        an unquiet mind
the halved soul gathering the light
from India to the planet Mars

you can get there from here
walking through walls, writing
down the bones
the new intelligence
a mother's journal breaking the code
 getting to yes, the city of yes
searching the skies
[for] near occasions of grace

Just Ask Her

his wife says she is the perfect victim
trapped by the extravagance of her own
philosophy, but listen:
                        she is a queen
                        bee, hived in a paper
                        room the size
                        of her marriage
she feeds her swarming children
loose food on sticky plates
she has exactly what she asked for
                        nothing
                        but the long
                        day long
                        to spend picking honey
                        from rough old scabs
these are brown paper coins she
can trade for love
such a languid, cranky invalid
sick from swallowing her own
potential
her chewing mouth, her pouches full,
                        she sucks up the hours
two cigarettes at a time
the sofa a warm caramel softening
into her bulbous shape

she calls for her mate
is he deaf?
the children are noisy, she's had no grapes
for the fruit bowl, and worse
the coffee has upset her again
look at him coming home from work
still in his boneless body
                        the sun is a gilded honey comb
                        slipping through her fingers,
                        its golden streak down
                        the nicotine window
                        mocking

her efforts to be patient
look how she narrows her glistening eyes,
her edges curl with disgust
surely he knows the difference between
rage and sadness
is   he   blind?
she has been   expecting
all day:
                        red and yellow petals,
                        a chunk of fragrant wax,
                        anything like a gift
she dares him
she double-dares him to come
on home, honey
just
try to make her smile

Pictures of Me Not Even Bothering:

I am the pile of bones I have to pick

a doctor of euphemisms calling
to say my mother no longer had a
p.u.l.s.e.
we were watching a stupid movie

overexposed images
from the hospital room
refer to my failed life
with her, you

a persistence of collapse

1
your hands on the telephone, the steering wheel
did not believe anyone could   die
not just from drinking a little scotch
and to prove it
you

invited your friend to come along
a child's tactic to un-death death

2
the room a still life:
the yellow blanket, the angle of the sun
and you, an excuse for a husband

you, with your back against
the farthest wall
death-fear lodged in your body
deep as a broken-off needle

and me there, too
performing the peculiar handshake
with the dead
your friend waiting awkwardly in the hall

3
your tawdry hands
busy
in the bathroom, the car, wherever
tweaking your own addictions
the trinity of them

shall I name them each
shall I tell?

4
how death made its fixed impression
in your eyes
caught you like an animal
on the wide open plain
of certainty

your neck twisting toward
the only window
that might let you go
back into summer
the green threshold of evening

5
your hands always on me
both hard and soft
but
always on me

the way they failed utterly
at simply failing

6
scaredy-man
I laughed at you
a little
from my bone-pile, held up
the ruined example of her body

see what happens?
when you wash your favourite shirt
on hot, leave the milk
out all night

you never believe anything
I tell you

A Consolation of Lilacs

~

no-one would call what we do
a visit—two skinny
women in a breathless room
me, medicated for a bad marriage
mother, just the bones stretched
out at one end of sleep
each of us pushing on
like an empty cargo ship

I come bearing a fistful
of lilacs, their stems seeping green
another gift of pineapple juice
warming in its foil box at the bedside
her book of crossword puzzles unfinished

~

this waiting has room
(to remember the taste of garden
raspberries mashed by sisters
and patted onto doll plates, sprinkled
with a crust of stolen sugar

our brother a clenched fist sound
asleep inside her

we imagined her recipe for pie, cut
silver dollar slices
of crab-apple, another crust of sugar
the sweet burn of cinnamon, also stolen)

~
she was drowning someone
steeping her in the sepia tea of disappearance

alone in her divorcee's apartment pouring out
the colours of glass and amber
she gives up answering, doesn't call
commits to her slow-handed suicide
then begins to die of drinking
of going under
years of too many fluids, then suddenly not enough

now, her body's mandate becomes refusal
its method desiccation, a hollow blowing away
irony's rusty dart splits me and I carry
its meaning home from the bedside
the boxes of pineapple juice
her watch on my wrist, her teeth
yes, in my purse

~
I cannot ask her
(what happened at her house on the farm
to that starved child she was, living
in the greenstick basket of her bones

the blue blades
of her grown-up lips made for hushing
her own pack of whelps
for reducing and paring
all activity to that of clear necessity
dishes washed, toys off the floor)

~

a room can be a continent of unasked questions
the notebook I find in her suitcase, a creasing
of memory, her whole life
she believed an uncle had fathered
her and some of the others, my mother's
mother then, a pitiless woman who kept
two men—brothers, farmers
tight in her chicken-killing grip

I keep a tearless vigil, chart only the medical facts
I need a four-letter word for sleep
c is for coma—a repose unlike any other
her breathing is a deep-seated machine
that takes time and swings it
rhythmically through her body

~

would she remember
(the three of us sent out
to play after a long morning's rain
she'd had enough racket for one day
we trooped out in our boots, straight
to the gardenside, stepped in like a chorus line
sank into the mud past our ankles
a meeting of scarecrows
sunflowers taking a vote
one of us had to step outside herself
walk the long wet lawn in sunlight
represent us in soaking wet kneehighs)

~
for the first and last time, we have a moment
of confluence
an eleventh-hour attempt at truth
possibly forgiveness
I know that she feels
something inside the brambled hedge
of disillusionment

in the waning light
what we are makes itself gently known to us

her hands, naked and painfully familiar
scrawling her secret on leaves of lined paper
a consolation
for going under, her pen a delirious instrument
suppressing the room of childhood

I begin a slow waking
as she sinks into her sleep
pending, womb-like in its yellow bed
with her pen I fill in the spaces
c is for commitment
I hear death standing quietly in the hall
its lesson for the month of June—patience
an edgeless shallow
sensation as green
as spring, as lilac as the inconsolable air

Her Dream Is the Water

my mother is submerged
a fetus in the sac of her illness

turns her head from side to side
all day
matting the back of her hair
she may be saying no

asks for green grapes
the fruit she asked for all her life
for the *sour* of them
squeeze them now
the juice falls into her falling mouth

this dying is slow and delirious
I must mother her body
without asking
       (ask her, go on)
if she was ever so kind to me

her dream is absolution
immersion
her dream is the water she breathes

small and afraid
she is
I am
still

membrane of amnesia
luminous, laid between
mother and child

this dying is done so fast
I won't turn one page
of the calendar
sit there or stand
every day in my shoes
my regular clothes

hold the bent straw
the water, the juice
untouched
hold
for the weight of
something in my hand

demand an explanation
where she's gone
is where she's always been
unreachable
the hardened pith of her heart
grape, gooseberry, crabapple

little fruit of sour water
she's gone under
mother her still
body gently

The Sky I've Made

Small Town Desire

when I was a girl I loved
a mannequin
a five-minute romance
that stung like bees
a flash hotter than the day
that pushed me into
the empty coolness of the store
        so boldly
mute was her invitation
I curved my hand on
the turned-over teacup
of her breast
not knowing
it was the hardest thing
I would ever touch
        I knew better
than to lift her asexual skirt
no dream of discovery
would lie folded
between her fibreglass thighs
I traced her frozen face
the wrongness of her terrible
hair like wires
placed over her averted glance
oh, I thought of her often
        in high school
as she recurred in the flesh
all around me
(too sexy in jeans
those implacable eyes
body supple as a vine
ready to climb some
brick wall of a guy)
        I never stopped
loving her though my lips were
sealed   my hand stalled
in a raised motion to caress
or merely ask a question

Termination of View 1

I don't mean to be sarcastic
I loved you, the two of us
arriving home

winter breath fluting in cold rooms
our care with molecules and kindling
allowing warmth its generosity

our hands consoling each other
with their deliberate acts

it was during the time we
imagined ourselves
urban rustic metro pioneers
so happily, gardeningly
married

oh
how we opposed
with our opposing theories
      sub
        urbia

two women
safe in our inner-city cedar-clad
its wood stove with every log
just the right length
split and corded by the classified-ad
woodsman

consider that cottage-ized city house
sporty car and camper
canoe used twice because I was afraid
suddenly
in that flimsy pod
of the dire-ness of lakes

yes that was our life

I keep my own ways now
have sunk below your sight-lines
      sub
        optic
conspicuous in my poverty

the words
rented, rust-bucket, second-hand
curl the pretty paint on your cross-town walls
flatten the tires of both your convertibles
render me a pathetic shiver
down your excellent spine

well, maybe a little sarcastic

Lesbian Scenarios You Don't Think About

my girlfriend had her back to me
doing dishes, and I said to her
so, would you like to see my wedding dress?
I had it dangling from my thumb
in its plastic
ten-year-old cocoon
she turned slowly, unsure

if she had heard correctly
her dark eyebrows incredulous
what? she said
*would you like to see my
wedding dress?* I repeated
she said she guessed so—

me being her first lover to arrive
with a trousseau
she waited with dripping hands
while I hung it on the fridge door
and showed her what I wore
(as someone else)
to a ritual of inertia

that carried my body ten years
through a minefield of denial
and mistaken identity
my great confusion that amuses her so
I told her I continue
to keep the dress
because the lace is valuable

because it feels like
(someone else's) amnesia
her only comment
perfect insertion of perspective
was that she was glad
it was only cocktail length

Your letter: 5 Translations

1. In which I remember everything you say

I fall asleep like a stone dropping
into stilled water

the body's revelation you said
is giving in to inertia

(understand)
by this you mean more than sleep

I fall
my wakefulness released

from fingers
that have forgotten to hold

(always)

there were the long ago messages
from the crows you promised to send

(still)

not one word from you
in your otherwise naked hand

2. Dream one: a coincidence of water

once, on the same night, we both dream a lake
my night's recurrent habit calling on you
from across town

I dream my old child-self
alone in a tipping canoe
the water turns over in its bed
and makes space for me
I roll in
my blonde hair stroked in the tepid embrace

such is the gentle violence of dreams

you visit the same lake, in your sleep's own season
it is winter
you are with a boy you cannot save
your two bodies break
through the bubble-flex of ice
you slide under, leaving no trace

these children sink my thought
of what is young in us, and in danger
our whole lives
a forensic analysis over the phone
        a retrospective drowning

3. Dreams two and three

~

a silver pouring of minnows from a bucket
a half-grown trout skitter-shining
from my hand

this could be you returning to the stream

in the morning
you say: dreams have no meaning
I say:
if a dreamwoman comes for you
your gesture of sleep, it means
what it means

~

pay attention, this is your dream
I'm dreaming:

a woman dressed in gauze
dances outside your window
the phosphoric glow of streetlamp
reveals her

she holds your silted body
like water in her cleft of hand
and you let her

bind your hands and feet
to the fretted corners of her heart
her tongue an imposition

its question moves you slowly
toward tears, toward
the seductive restraint

of her demand
calls
your body away from me

I am answering your letter, or she is
with her semaphore
my words travel through the night

4. Reading what has gone unwritten

it is clear you meant to write—
our recipe for dinner, the distillation
of your intent (in the form of a list)
an annotated diagram showing
the collapsing aperture of your leaving

don't kiss me, ever
I am an opinion based on conjecture
your touch guessing
which, of all the bodies, should be mine
I have never been less beautiful
my voice b-flat, a dial-tone

this message will be waiting for you
when you finish walking home
from wherever it is
you take yourself
when you appear
the way objects appear from fog
that sudden
lack of invisibility
this message will be waiting:

darling, raven-head
I will become harder to please

5. What doesn't kill me

you fall asleep without falling
even the distance of a single breath

your sleep, a suddenly still
photograph of you gone from your body

I describe your sleeping as:
an absence smaller than exhalation

nearly fallen,
a bird lighting without its weight

a pause
next to the corrugation of my body

my missing body
your letter answered

Some Notes Toward Drowning

what it sounds like when I lie awake wondering:
you move from room to room
downstairs, speak to each cat in her language

you are at the bottom of a slow river
lit with streetlight, our rooms the colour of tea
I held a poem all day like a crushed

tissue in an old woman's fretting hand
words that separate your intent
from my longing

coming home before you, the place I came from
not yet a memory, not yet a beginning
above you I pretend to have slept—frustrated

my guts a burning boat
all my old hungers wide awake
and full of questions

flooded in this blue room, by this city's blue-lit
idea of darkness
across my skin, my hand

remembers touch, so little too late
far below me
I hear you moving stones

The Middles of Our Conversations

9.   you
       broke my heart
       with wanting
8.   you lifted me
       let me live with you
       in that anarchy of bliss
7.   shopping. I could go on
       it's always the simple things
       one misses
6.   all the first times you brought
       to my sheltered life, girl
       sex words talking hard
       and rude big bountiful
       food and beer the green
       green water tree world
5.   everything. oh yes, I was
       wolfgirl lifted from the wild
       don't think I don't appreciate
4.   you kept giving me my self
       my self, a redundant gift
       but you never stopped giving
3.   though I still believe
       there are some lies in
       love with you
2.   I've lived a whole lifetime
       in five minutes under your wing
       I'm catching up to myself, breathless
1.   of course it means something
       but it doesn't have to be
       regret

Return Address

it was easy then, when our bodies did the talking

my unscented skin was a trick
of sunlight and loofa
the slatted blinds over our bed
tilted the blue remains of light

my relentless questions, your imperfect evasions
        a form of courtship

these days I am confused in the folds
of what is and is   not
left to us

it's true
we've had no Paris, no Venice
but I've been to Florence (without you)
know the statue of David
is much larger than an ordinary man
        I am resigned to such empty statements

how does one declare love without body, chisel or pen?

I've stolen myself
a small gift, a spectrum of lilies
they smell of something animal, like meat
or skin or maybe
rotting pears, but not of flowers
as we like to imagine them

certain things in love are obvious
you say   I say
the way to the end is scattered
with other people's gardens

in your exhausted luggage was a plain
girl folded in
her skin, like trousers or a linen shirt
waiting (she knew my name)
waiting like she might be worn

I still have questions
I remain a curious girl though
the words are far behind me now

these days, I imagine
you as you were
smelling of thin perfection, smelling of
sandalwood or paper
without words

your creaking blue
chairs and cardboard couch
I close my eyes and remember
how I was a message mixed
in your overwhelming strata of papers

your many departures and arrivals

now I find
I've gone the way of the afternoon (sunset
a trick of pinks and blues)
the way of the lilies—
their afterthought of beauty
a state of anxious decay

like a hand full of stems
opening
I begin to let you go

and you leave me
not even an old shopping list to treasure
the indifference of your handwriting
just an impression
left
indented on my imagination:
darling,
    I've gone for the milk
(its perfect translucence)
but promise to return

Termination of View 2

but I loved you, as I said
your hair like crow feathers
tossing off light like droplets of water

the old blue-stoned ring
you let me keep
(off-handed though our last
conversation was)

because it matched inconceivably
my mother's wedding band

because it was gold
that had learned to live in peace
with my cheap silver rings
the whole extended family of them

our houseful of purchases
split, zygotic
into two new lives
our sadness the last thing
we would agree on

the cat had died of cancer
(or the surgery to save him)
and there was nothing left
to fight over
nothing left standing
you said, between us
and divorce

Epilogue:

this is the sky I've made
visceral and tumbling
clear, unbearably
in the distance

I ask nothing of you now
my sadness is like motherhood:
a structure built of forfeit
our evicted bodies

their eloquent gestures of retreat
are behaving as though
wakened from a dream
remember me in mid-turn

imagine our life

grasp the water
that has made us a bridge
how once a digression like that

could have changed everything

I won't tell you where
but there is a beach
near here

with a million
heart-shaped stones
in her hair

Bloodblossom

Line of Questioning

tell me about yourself, how colour speaks
itself to you, do you notice the blue

of sky when it leans over you
transparent and crisp as cellophane

do you notice the way it punctures
and collapses, the blue, like a breath on

the tips of the distant pine
also, if a woman dreams you

where on her body would you first
place your hand, do you see

how like a heartbeat on a paper
strip this horizon is

I'm only asking, or the green when you travel
through it from some city-dweller's metaphor

for silence, the blue everywhere it fuses
with the million shades of green

do you wonder, in your concrete city
if it is blue/green

or green/blue that merge like lovers
just beyond the grey

tell me what word
do you type on your naked

document—turquoise or aqua
the difference is desire, it is viewpoint

Stealing Mercury

~

it's nothing to want, the science teacher had said
just moments before I became a thief:
        dead of winter, earth had turned
        its back to the sun
to me in the skinny lab
that was once a cloakroom

        in my bare hand
my stolen drop of mercury
and somewhere behind me
the teacher's blind eye as I poured

~

does it matter what I call myself?
my constant
question has taken us, you and me
the amalgam of our day to day
engulfed our conversation in the dark
woods of desiring the difficult
makes me ask again

and again if it's you I want
a man   (the flats of your body
                    a field of muscle
                    a landscape of pelt)
or a woman to sleep with—me the curve
her absolute correlation, the nest

does it matter that I am two animals?
yearning   fugitive
loitering   overfed
a crossword creature

what matters is
that I sleep with you

that you are nest enough
gravity has taken us and
made us applicable (your body a bone forest
                    a swaying of branches
                    between me and the stars)

~

desire is persistent matter
a heavy metal moving like an animal
under the skin
I want some things just because
they are beautiful

a small drop of mercury
colder than a planet
a living bead in the cup of my mitten-less
hand an offering to the weather
to the protector of children
from poison and frostbite

the earth and its winter
day sliding into dark, like liquid
silver into a bottle

Starting Now

I said that desire had long passed
through me
        a tracer bullet
dragging proof of its flight through the air
its strings of light dangling
        off the edge of my teetering world
that love was what one could tolerate
forever stretched out like a cat
blind eyelid lifting in an ecstasy of lapse
it's too easy to get tangled, caught
in a life infected and re-infected
with its burden of lies
watch how the world convolutes itself
around its own suffering
it has always been this way
it has always been this amazing
how hungry the body can be
how damaged, and yet still live

then you show up in your peaceful attire
contradicting me with your unbound silences
you take me walking through the fluid
dynamics of this city
which, like me, is thawing and beginning again
in spring the swift river
its ridiculous balance of water and ice
moves in the only direction
I argued there was no point in a garden
an old house in an old neighbourhood
succumbing to time's impoverishments
no point in one small hour beside a lake
(its green sweater and shoes full of stones)

you said look
the birds lift themselves up
without surprise
go
where they need to go
it has always been this easy
I move toward yes, let you take me
to the edge of the water
yes, I want what they want
I see the bouquets of them
softly opening and closing

There Have Been Mornings Like This

when I go without breakfast
        to the vast grey patio
        of the lake and stand, abject—
        as city people often are—
        in the frank adjudication of sunrise

when you think I have told you everything
        because we knelt in this bed
        envisioning the electrified sky
        purple and rainless through the window
        and I imagined it was 1999, or any year
        a war we could see
        repeating itself just over the horizon

when I stagger out of my sleep
        the thing I did not tell you
        already risen and making coffee
        the lightning storm a memory, my shape
        matted into the body of the bed
        and yes, there you are
        still beautiful

when the sun, from behind the lake
        is a blonde head emerging
        from the cowl of a silver sweater
        and I don't know what else to do
        with my stubborn, loving body
        but teach it to see

Verge

you fill me up the way the arm of river fills its long sleeve
a longitudinal extension of energy that carries me
to the end of who I am
when I leave you for the open road you say
don't go
but I drive on, as I must
my lap a fruit basket, our dialogue interrupted
the red taste of cherries replacing you in my mouth
birch and poplar stand to their ankles

in floodwater, whispering directions
this far, and no farther

our words open holes beneath our feet
some declarations we've made leave us
standing over air
denial, like heavy fog, moves in to fill the voids
to prevent a fall
through gravity, through this city, its episodes
of raining and embedded light
we are kept apart by fronts of invisible pressures

by recorded messages that tell us
what we can reasonably expect

I'm trying to say something about love
how it sees me in my kitchen slicing lemons
pressing hot water from spinach, the bowl
I press within the sieve, a skull
fitted neatly into its scalp
attentive to this meal I repeat from memory
I pretend that loving you is incidental
an accidental bending of logic

yet its inflection moves in me
fixes me in the frame of its longing

a step ahead of me, my body
has left you a message
what we see, filtered and oblique
each from our separate windows, I describe as a season
but is merely light
on its way through things
a slice of lemon in a glass of water
the overlapping green textile of early summer

green so full of yellow it lifts us
from the moment

Two Solitudes

are you bored with me yet, he asked?

        with his body I am learning
        to understand, its forest and
        silt deposits
        with his lesbian hands
        with his not being
        a girl

        with our conversations, whispered
        though we are each alone
        in our unmade beds
        the phone cord spooling into the sheets

my body has conspired against me
surprised me once and for all

I describe my life as a series of
confessions
I mean, concessions
all my memories have been
drained and exiled
to the island of apples and oranges

I want him to be the one
I do not injure
with my body
I am learning to understand
the fine line I walk, a blade

not yet, I tell him
not yet

My Morning Body

you are sleeping past sunrise
(curled between hither and yon)
when I finish a book written by a man, at once
poetic and unafraid

I say to the silence what women will say
(lips seeking the white curve)
when nudged open
when slaked with words

love me like the first time I touched your skin
(poetic and unafraid)
my thumbnail gentle beside your lips
its parabolic curve recognizing

the shape of a scar I did not give you
(you are sleeping)
I've kissed you now and kissed you since, my
lips seeking the white curve

between hither and yon
read aloud the shape of my want
(when nudged open) awake
my morning body folded over you
like feathers

Bloodblossom

it's like this in October, driving east to Winnipeg
this stretch of highway a back and forth scar
I've scratched into the earth my whole life
ditches waist-high with escaped domestics and weeds
early snow dusts the dead fields
I'm looking for the only tree for miles
still wearing its leaves like a tattered bloody coat
a tree not from around here—immigrant, shy
not ready for the early nakedness of trees in these parts
the only shred of colour in an hour of miles

a rip in the prairie monochrome
standing there like love exposing its vein to the wind

yesterday I headed west
to the scene of my adolescence
drove past an old memory of black ice
my first car sliding efficiently into the ditch
packed snow the only view from a nose-dive
perspective, pretzels and coffee
spackling the inside of the car
but that was years ago
before you were chipped whole
from the limestone depths of my life

before you began waiting for me to return
from everywhere and find you home

it's like Cinderella, that sugar maple far from home
an embarrassment of colour
in a deserted ballroom
bloodblossom, ruby, corpuscle
still wearing last night's velvet
the party well over
you love me like that, isolated and radiant
or maybe that's how I love you
like waking from a dream
of red in a white field

like fire's convicted memory
in the empty arms of the trees

The Animals That Inhabit Him

The Animals That Inhabit Him

~

it's true I've gone deaf these many weeks
temporary, ear-infected solitary

confinement
a near total blotting out of sound

but what is lost is not the point
       he has his own wounds

voices are bees
circling the sweet gardenias of my ears

I find my way along the map of veins
I see below his skin

~

this is his body
long
tall
clad in black
he is my child

he cannot scare me
       walking out like that

across the half-frozen
flung arm of river
tourniquets and used syringes
       sinking along
the soft taunt of its edge

his father's new marriage
has no room for him

this is our street
the number on our house
as it appears on his library card
attendance record

he attaches himself like a shard
to the place he refers to as home

~

he passes silently through my silent rooms
inferring a loss of all my senses:

my eyes blind, my fingers reading
between the lines

lone dog
followed by the black wraith of his hair

he is
his own familiar

the street is a river

in the dark of it
his long black coat was lifted from his shoulders
at the point of a knife

  it was just a guy, mom
it was nothing
took his half-pack of smokes and his bus pass

I query him in the motherly way
my deafened head a packed
and baffled wound

~

if I tied him down
to keep him home
he would bleed
  a red word
he would be
crimson and black at the points
of tethering

hemophilic,
his blood tries to love him

an entrepreneur,
it begins expansion in the joints
         knee as big as a head
an artist, it opens
its blood bouquets
behind the shifting scrim
of his skin

he keeps a katana beneath his futon mattress
a Japanese warrior, sword at the ready
the jungle of his basement
room
bruised
his curtains
slashed to ribbons

~

the street is not enough
the river is an open vein

every night
he climbs to the top of the city

part insect
gracile

thin boots and fingertips learning
the scrupulous language

of architecture, engineering:
dormer, cornice, girder and rung

he is a crow, eating the wind
washing his eyes with stars

he has a message for his father—
the weight of this emptiness lifts him

~
little boy on a gurney
butterfly pinned to a board

learned early that pain
(accidental, inflicted)
must always be followed by pain
(injected, infused)

hematoma

an active bleed

looks like a flower
like a fried egg
hot to the touch
surreal and alive in purple
cherry red spreading

at its centre—calcium, salt
      a hard white heart
a human stone

~
the river is:

a calamity in slow motion

a withering arterial stream

a trough of bristling blackened trees
on the deathbed of this glacial lake

        his city, a corruption of stone

~

his chance to write his memoirs
is endangered
with every midnight climb

he is last sighted
at the periphery of my silence

he is the raccoon
living under the back step
vexing me with nightly
cross examinations of the lawn
corners of fresh sod folded back
like so many black dinner napkins

he is darkness on the move
eating my leftovers
after I've gone to bed

the whorl of my unsleeping body
a shift in the soft
collapse of night

~

you can't tell by looking at me:
my head is a worry room
      (he cannot scare me)
it is packed and baffled against
sound, against reason

I query him
(it's the motherly way)
ask him to repeat his answers, repeat
himself, his words
repeat
and in this way we have entire
conversations

I ask if he's heard from his father

sealed in my temporary
deafness, I am
a closed head wound
closed-head
head-wound

~
the river did not want him
without his coat
without the weight
of his preoccupations

whether we are the living
or the dying
the point is not loss, it is
the fellowship loss brings

~
I do not tell him
my fear is like a disease
(he cannot scare me, my mantra)

my insomnia is deaf
to the reasonable argument of sleep
my deafness is wide awake and
expecting the police

      when he is home
I track his movements with my eyes
there he is
in the tv's underwater flicker
silent
again, always
his grasshopper body filling the entire couch

eyes of an animal, warning me off

~
our dialogue is a contest of wills
        my demand
that he keep his feet on the ground
        his desire
to climb the night like a spider on a thread

yet we are fragile, consumed
each in our own country of isolation

injured and scarred, we wait
for the next affliction
to find us
each surprisingly unprepared
for the other

the margin of such care
is not without confinement

~

on the smooth soles of his old
black army boots
he arrives at a certain conclusion

        he walks out of my home

if he doesn't have a father
he will have nothing—

where does that leave
me. me. me.

leaves me
stifled in my armchair

this is not grieving
this early spring

this waking, uselessly
at sunrise

the scudded trails of clouds
point the direction
he took through me

~

this riverbottom where I live

I have forgotten
my desire to be heard

forgotten
what sound tastes like

he cannot scare me—
green blur of light's broken

arm as it passes
through me

he cannot scare me
(my mantra)

~

the question I ask:
if I make him a nice dinner
if he comes home to eat it
will it keep him alive?

the hum of the fridge is muffled
the chaos of wondering where he is
deafens my hunger
hungers my sleep

the answer he gives:
death—zero
him—fifteen

he is constantly returning
from death's country

~

one day while driving I see
a pack of crows, one after another
landing on the street between speeding cars

they come in like rescue-choppers, like
a handful of thrown coins
metallic throats reporting murder—
a murder in the whizzing middle of traffic
their fallen comrade blown down, swerved
open, black as a burst tire

I do not tell him
it was him my imagination saw
torn black coat in the road

~

at times I find him still a part of me
remaindered, circling,
still   apart of me

the length of his back
as he turns it to me
a beaded wire

one vertebra for each year
he has endured
inside his skin

there is nothing to be done but wait
the polluted shells of my ears
feel only the rushing of wind or water

or blood, its red cable
tapping out a signal
comehome   comehome

~

every morning the river wakes up
in a new place
the only constant is its temporary address

its give and take
he moves along the oblique angle
of his shadow, tending toward escape

relinquishes everything:
his guitar, his birthday presents
the currency of his resolve
to keep moving

pawned for a package of noodles

~

the night sky eats my composure
under its expressionless eye I flail

sure, a father should know his son—
should listen at night to the twisting

of his heart in its deep red washing machine
should know what it is to wait up for his child

to imagine the uniform at the door
with the news

      fallen this time
a dark shape on a gurney

the burst balloon
of his body

~

I do not tell him
one of his familiars has come to me
small shadow of consolation

a foundling in my garden
a plea
stubborn little goat

stands with her forehead
pressed against the door till I open it
once and for all

her black fur shot through with
single white hairs
she loves me

this cat in my lap
her black fur
a transfusion
a sudden constellation

~
I ask him where he spends his nights
the bus depot
instant bank machines
boiler rooms in public buildings
boarded-up houses
heated bus shacks
the airport

foundling—
this kind of sleeping, hungry

and bent
in the warm armpits of the street

its sweaty pockets,
is named Vagrancy

the wind's lewd finger
up the pant-leg, up the sleeve

blood feeling out the terrain
of his concrete bed

when they find him under the stairs
he gives the police his father's address

~
he moves through the bloodless
streets of the city's old body
he is held in its loose grid
of tendon, sinew, teeth
even in the dark the city does not sleep

knows I hear
what I want to hear
in the absolute room of my head:
       his keys opening the lock
          the ransom for his safe return paid
a tympanic distortion of night

~

why, when he first leapt
in me, a butterfly
in a cup,
did I make no preparation for loss?

my uncomplicated craving to make
something of my own
a child that would never leave me
then yes,
young muscles (opened)
around a reddened silence
made

a space for him

gave him the dubious gift
of my cells, a failure
of the blood, its one missing factor

the warp and weft of what is wrong in each of us
our future contingent

in my head, a picture
wrapped in darkness:

his body
a spool of veins
        unravelling

~

from what source a message
he will hear?

he writes himself into the margin
of his story

whatever this is—
undertow or forced march

his monologue of silence
how can I give him anything?

Acknowledgements

Grateful thanks to The Manitoba Arts Council for financial help that allowed me the time to go the distance from a stack of papers to a manuscript, to Sarah Klassen for our time as mentor and apprentice, to Melanie Cameron for reading the first, far too long, version, George Amabile for a thorough cross-examination of an earlier incarnation of "The Animals That Inhabit Him." To the editors of the following journals and the anthology in which variations of some of these poems appeared: *Contemporary Verse 2, dark leisure, Other Voices,* and *Prairie Fire*; *Body Language: a Head to Toe Anthology* (Black Moss Press), and the authors of all the books mentioned in the poem "Mother Road."

Special thanks to writers group members and good friends Robyn Maharaj, Sharon Caseburg, Clarise Foster and to former members Kathie Axtell and Lisa Petite—for the years of invaluable critiques, support and advice, to my family for never being too far away and for the stories, to Eileen Agar, my longest friend, for the line in "Return Address", to Jocelyn Beaudette for her unconditional support of my early writing and without whose prompting it might never have left the nest and to Nora Schwetz, Nurse Coordinator, for being only a phone call away for 21 years, or my son's entire life, whichever way you look at it, and for giving me the book *Raising a Child with Hemophilia: A Practical Guide for Parents* by Laureen A. Kelley, from which the found poem by the same title originated.

Particular thanks to Jody Hudey for her creative instinct, her interpretation of my sensibility and for composing the perfect cover image, to Jusstice Musseau for wearing that size-too-small dress all day on a windy rooftop without complaining once, and to Clarise's ubiquitous biker jacket for agreeing to appear on my book cover. To my publisher Gord Shillingford of The Muses' Company and Karen Green for all their hard work on my behalf. To Catherine Hunter, my editor, for her absolutely uncompromising eye, for helping me simultaneously sculpt the work as though it were clay and sharpen it as though it were steel and for the pleasure of working together, and to friend, poet and editor Clarise, for the submitted version of the manuscript, and for the writerly talks that kept me off the figurative ledge.

Enduring thanks to: my son, Linden Paine, for walking his own path, always, for teaching me to be a grown-up, for the inevitable material, and for continuing to make it safely home each night. And to Todd Besant, for every part of our life together as companions, friends, writers.